How to Be a More Effective Group Communicator

How to Be a More Effective Group Communicator

*Finding Your Role and
Boosting Your Confidence
in Group Situations*

Deborah Shouse

SkillPath Publications
Mission, Kansas

Project Editor: Kelly Scanlon

Editor: Jane Doyle Guthrie

Book Design: Premila Malik Borchardt and Rod Hankins

Cover Design: Rod Hankins

Library of Congress Catalog Card Number: 95-71778

ISBN: 1-57294-016-6

10 9 8 7 6 5 4 3   01 02 03 04

Printed in the United States of America

Contents

Introduction

You're part of a special project team...you're lunching with other department heads...you're facilitating a strategic planning session...you're attending an all-day workshop...you're organizing this year's company party... Every day, whether you're conscious of it or not, you play different roles in different groups of people—family, friends, neighbors, and business associates.

In fact, success in the workplace increasingly hinges on your ability to function and flourish in groups. With new situations today often come new challenges with new groups of colleagues. Thus, no matter how competent, how innovative, how specialized you are, you will be more successful and ultimately more valuable to your organization when you feel comfortable in teams, committees, business units, and other group situations.

2

When you're at ease and effective in group interactions, you increase your visibility as well as your ability to understand and work with people. In addition, you heighten your sense of confidence and esteem, certainly a bonus if not already one of your goals!

How to Be a More Effective Group Communicator gets you started developing your group self—whether as a participant or a leader. The discussion and exercises that follow offer you easy opportunities to learn more about yourself and to become an accomplished, valued partner in the group process.

one

Discovering Your Group Role

A s a youngster, George had a traumatic first year in Cub Scouts. While the other boys were trooping through the woods, identifying animal tracks and finding nuts and berries to eat, George hid behind a tree, clutching his inhaler and hoping to ward off an asthma attack. Even though these scouting nightmares occurred years ago, George still gets attacked by what he terms "troop group fear." If he's around people he doesn't feel comfortable with, he clams up and isolates himself.

Anna was a leader in both high school and college. As a legal secretary, she feels comfortable with her co-workers, clients, and bosses. She also feels free to speak out and direct any group she's part of, even when it's not appropriate.

Who are you in a group? Have you ever analyzed your own "herd" instincts? For example, are you the faithful sheep dog, herding everyone together and keeping them on course? A lost lamb merely following the crowd? A wolf in sheep's clothing, hiding among your colleagues?

Visualize the scenarios in Exercise #1 to help you put a face on your group I.D.

Ex**erc**i**se** #**1**:
Discovering Your Group I.D.

1. It's 8:10 a.m., ten minutes past the scheduled starting time. You and six other members of the visioning team stand around, trying not to yawn. Brad, the facilitator, hasn't arrived and neither has the coffee. You check your watch and:

   A. Worry you won't get to your next meeting on time.

   B. Call Brad's office to see how you can help get things started.

   C. Applaud when Ann says, "Who wants coffee and what kind?" Volunteer to help her.

   D. Make a mental note that this is the third time Brad has been late for a meeting and wonder how his lateness can benefit you.

2. "Any questions?" the speaker asks. The room of twenty has the energy of a noonday tomb. You know your boss spent a lot of money bringing in this speaker, and your company is expecting great things from this training session. You:

   A. Wonder who will ask the first question.

   B. Quickly glance at your notes, raise your hand, and ask the speaker to amplify the last point.

   C. Wait and see how smart the other questions are before you decide whether to speak out.

   D. Frame a question you think the speaker will find difficult to answer.

3. Your company is small, with a staff of only five people. The office manager prides herself on holding problem-solving sessions every Friday afternoon. Today you are exhausted—you had a week full of problems and you don't feel like discussing them. Apparently, no one else does either. The manager begins to look upset. She asks for issues and everyone just stares at their hands. You:

A. Stare at your watch and notice it needs cleaning.

B. Say, "I've had such a complex week that I'm too exhausted to pour energy into problem solving. Is there a chance we can reconvene Monday morning?"

C. Hope that Norton is his usual outspoken self. Once he gets started, you'll manage to chime in.

D. Hope that no one talks so the manager will forget this obsession with group process and let everyone go on home.

4. You recently volunteered to help a local charity put on a fund-raising party. At the first planning session, you realize that the group members all know each other. You feel like a first grader at the junior high dance. You:

A. Wait for someone to notice you and draw you into the conversation.

B. Say, "I'd like to meet everyone. Can we all introduce ourselves?"

C. Wait until everyone has volunteered for something before you raise your hand.

D. Think, "I knew volunteer groups were cliquish and disorganized."

5. Your professional organization is holding its monthly luncheon meeting. You arrive late and grab the last seat at a table for five. You try not to frown as you realize what the lively conversation is centered around: cats. You are here for networking and business information. Besides, cats make you sneeze. You:

A. Listen in case someone tells an interesting story.

B. Say, "Speaking of cats, what have you learned from your pets that applies to the business world?"

C. Wait for someone to change the subject, then gratefully jump in.

D. Say, "Cats make me sneeze. I don't know what people see in them."

In the situations where you answered "A," you were a watcher and observer, reluctant to step out of the herd. When you chose "B," you showed leadership skills. "C's" indicate a readiness to follow, once someone else has smoothed out the rough edges. Beware the wolf in corporate clothing: When you answered "D," you were lurking around thinking negative thoughts.

You won't act the same in every group. Your contributions will vary according to environment, number of people, seating arrangements, and purpose of the gathering. Your past experiences in groups also affect your attitude today.

Part of getting great with groups is understanding your natural strengths and tendencies. Find out more about where you are now by completing the self-portrait in Exercise #2.

Exercise #2:
Finding Your Group Strengths and Weaknesses

1. Think of a group situation where you felt totally at ease.
Write down the things that made you feel good.

Examples
- "The group was small."
- "The meeting was less than two hours."
- "We had no structure."
- "We started on time."

_____

_____

_____

_____

What did you like about the people in this group?

Examples
- "I knew everyone."
- "We were all from the same city."
- "We were all the same gender."

_____

_____

_____

_____

What did you like about your behavior in this group?

Examples

- "I was natural."

- "I knew a lot."

- "I felt good facilitating."

_____

_____

2. Now remember a situation where you felt like a person without a country. Write down the elements that made you feel uneasy: _____

_____

_____

What was difficult about the people? What about your behavior was displeasing to you?

Examples

- "I can't believe I talked so much."

- "I didn't say a word the whole time."

_____

_____

_____

3. Look again at the group situations you examined in items 1 and 2. What can you learn from each? _____

_____

_____

_____

Discovering Your Group Role

10

4. List your strengths in a group:

   Examples
   - "I'm good with strangers."
   - "I'm quick on my feet."

   _____

   _____

   _____

5. List the areas you want to work on: _____

   _____

   _____

6. List all the groups you currently attend. Include work, family, social, and civic groups, as well as informal groups such as friends who gather once a month or a group that eats lunch together. Describe your role in each. Would you like to have a different role?

   Group 1 _____

   Your role _____

   Your dream role _____

   Group 2 _____

   Your role _____

   Your dream role _____

   Group 3 _____

   Your role _____

   Your dream role _____

Group 4 _____

Your role _____

Your dream role _____

Group 5 _____

Your role _____

Your dream role _____

Group 6 _____

Your role _____

Your dream role _____

Group 7 _____

Your role _____

Your dream role _____

Group 8 _____

Your role _____

Your dream role _____

Group 9 _____

Your role _____

Your dream role _____

Group 10 _____

Your role _____

Your dream role _____

7. Identify three groups you belong to that are stress free, where you feel comfortable and willing to make mistakes:

_____

_____

_____

8. Now set a goal for each group, some way you want to improve your performance in that group. Give yourself a fixed period of time for achieving your goal.

Examples

• "Learn something new about each group member."

• "Ask for help."

• "Change the subject gracefully when I feel bored."

Group 1 _____

Goal _____

Time Frame _____

Group 2 _____

Goal _____

Time Frame _____

Group 3 _____

Goal _____

Time Frame _____

Group 4 _____

Goal _____

Time Frame _____

*Group 5*_____

Goal _____

Time Frame _____

*Group 6*_____

Goal _____

Time Frame _____

*Group 7*_____

Goal _____

Time Frame _____

*Group 8*_____

Goal _____

Time Frame _____

*Group 9*_____

Goal _____

Time Frame _____

*Group 10*_____

Goal _____

Time Frame _____

14

Re-grouping

- Your contributions to the group will vary according to the environment, number of people, seating arrangement, and purpose of the group.

- Your past experiences in groups affect your attitude today.

- It helps to notice the roles you play and the roles you want to play in the groups you belong to.

How to Be a More Effective Group Communicator

two

Who's Who and What's What in a Group

The CEO has sent you a memo requesting your presence at a team-building seminar. The once positive atmosphere in the company has been overtaken by rumors and anxiety—your secretary believes your department is facing cutbacks, and various co-workers are concerned about possible mergers. You feel the company can't continue profitably without radical internal changes.

The seminar hasn't started when you arrive, but there's plenty of conversation going on. Two people you don't recognize are huddled in the corner, earnestly gesturing. Another is fiddling around at the coffeepot. Three are already seated, pens and

16

notebooks out. A woman wearing a guest badge is at the head of the table, stacking paper, testing markers, making sure everything is ready.

You are giving a sales presentation to the top management of a potential new client. You've worked with Hal, the client's director of marketing, but you've never met the others who'll be attending. Although you asked for biographies and background information on the CEO, CFO, and director of human resources and training, the marketing director provided only the most cursory paragraphs. You aren't even totally clear about who the decision maker is.

As you set up your slides and organize your handouts, seven people stroll into the room. Hal introduces you, but you can't tell by the titles who's who or what's what.

You've been asked to take part in the community focus committee at work. The group's task is to find worthy causes and plan a contribution to the community. This is a new group, and the only person you know is a public relations assistant who talks too much. You'd like this group to make a good name for your company and make a difference in the community.

Read Individual Barometers

Who's a leader and who's a follower? Who likes to sabotage and who likes to facilitate? Whether you're leading a group, sitting in with a group, or taking part in an ongoing team, you'll benefit from the "What's My Line" method of scoping out group members. A quick study of individual barometers such as body language, voice tone, and verbal context allows you to better survive in the group. "People often lose power in groups when they don't watch and listen," says Connie Russell, a psychotherapist with a specialization in career counseling.

From pirates to pioneers, people in potential conflict situations often posted a lookout to assess the scene. Be your own lookout and see who's guarding the fort, who's trying to invade, and who's off trying to establish some trading opportunities. Observing group dynamics *before* you plunge in too deeply strengthens your chances of being effective.

Besides developing an awareness of others, remember that you too are part of the "who's who and what's what" wondering going on in the room. There are two important strategies you can adopt in projecting well to your audience:

1. **Get the lead by beginning offstage.** John is always rushing into group gatherings at least ten minutes late. Pens fall from his notebooks, papers slide out of his hands. He bursts into the room in a blur of mumbled apologies and flying paper clips. If John had a comic role in a play, this entrance would be great, but it's disastrous if he wants to take a leading man position in his company.

When you rush in like John, you draw unflattering attention to yourself. People make a mental note of you as a blur of anxiety and manic energy. Worse, they see you before you have a chance to see them.

Walk into the room at a confident pace. Entering a meeting place is like walking on stage, so be ready for your audience. Be prepared to be seen and noticed. Don't fumble in your purse or pockets for a pen. Don't smooth your hair or adjust your clothing. Act like the poised star you want to be.

2. Carefully choose where to sit—don't hide in the balcony. As a newly promoted manager, Shelley wasn't sure how to act at the upcoming interdepartmental meeting. A little nervous when she walked in, she immediately saw three women she knew and joined them, relieved to find colleagues she was comfortable talking to. As the other managers entered, though, she noticed them taking seats nearer the speaker. She also noticed that she was sitting with a group of assistants rather than managers.

You've heard of power walking, power lunches, power tools, and power plays. When you can't be the chairperson, get your own power seat by choosing your spot carefully. Enhance your purpose and agenda by also carefully selecting *when* you sit. That is, if everyone is mingling, don't be the first to diffuse the energy and sit down.

It's tempting to be like Shelley and find the first friendly face to sit next to. But consider your business purpose: How do you want to be seen?

Once you're in the room, take a few moments to look around. Don't rush to a seat. Analyze the setting. Notice who's talking to whom. Who's sitting and who's standing? Are the power people sitting together? Are the people from lower management positions seated together? Where will the leader or facilitator be sitting?

Look at the room and think about where you want to be. What sitting position would be most advantageous? Meetings aren't like movie theaters, where you file in and sit anywhere as long as you can see. Ask yourself what your role is in the meeting. For example, when you're supporting the facilitator, sit across from that person. When you represent an opposing position, choose your seat accordingly.

"I always try to sit where I can see people and also be located near the leader," says Connie Russell.

Group Roles: Beauty and the Beast?

Sure, these are the same people you see at the computer, in the restroom, in the lunchroom. But somehow, in meetings and other group gatherings, people act out certain roles. Observe the following cast members in your group:

- **Yes and again yes! The Co-Leader.** This informal leader supports the facilitator. He or she often answers questions readily and articulately, emphasizing points the leader was trying to make. This role-player gives the group parameters and acknowledges contributions.

- **Prove it! The Skeptic.** "That will never work. We've always done it this way."

  The Skeptic can be a nightmare or an asset. She may strengthen the group with her questions, or he may irritate them with his objections. Besides impeding change, The Skeptic adds a conservative and generally resistive element to the group.

- **Look at ME! The Mascot.** "Have you heard the one about...?" "What you're saying reminds me of the time when my wife and I..."

  Besides having a lively personality and a generous smile, the Mascot tends to go overboard with stories that ramble and get off-track. This person's touches of levity often distract from the serious meat of the meeting.

- **Wonderful! The Sycophant.** For this cast member, everything the facilitator does is perfect. The Sycophant only has eyes for authority and tends to parrot the leader's line. Don't confuse this role with that of The Co-Leader, who offers substance to the proceedings by taking a supportive stance.

- **Unplucked and unplucky: The Wallflower.** "Was Susan at the meeting? I didn't see her. I don't remember a thing she said. Are you sure she was really there?"

  Ever feel like you're in a fog at a meeting? Ever want to disappear into the swivel chair? Although you may sometimes have days when your "hidden agenda" is simply to hide, group interaction and progress depends on participants, not observers. Wallflowers affect the energy and mood of the group.

  Giving yourself a chance to listen is not being a Wallflower, however—sometimes the smartest, most powerful people are quiet in meetings, and for good reasons. They speak up and get noticed only when they have something important to say.

Each of these characters has important characteristics that add to the group dynamic. Notice who contributes what. Particularly in ongoing groups, pay attention to how positions change. Remember that a person who sits in an opened relaxed fashion may be relaxed or may actually be fuming. Keep a constant watch on body language so you get the deeper meaning.

Complete Exercise #3 to get a handle on the roles people play in your groups.

Exercise #3:
Group Game Plan

Use this form as a guide for the next gathering you attend. If you are part of an ongoing group, copy the form and fill it out several times so you can document how the dynamics change. After you observe the members of a group, you're better positioned to make your own plan.

1. Notice who's seated and who's standing when you enter the room. What are their positions? (Use names if it's helpful.)

   Seated: _____

   _____

   _____

   Standing: _____

   _____

   _____

2. Notice the conversational groups. Are managers just talking to managers? Are the conversational circles interdepartmental? Are people discussing business or social items?

   • Departments seem to stick together: Yes   No

   • Positions seem to flock together: Yes   No

   • Conversations are: Business   Social   Mixture

   • Other: _____

3. Notice the seating arrangement.

- Who sits on either side of the leader? (Write down their positions and names.) _____

  _____

- Who sits across from the leader? _____

  _____

- Who sits farthest away from the leader? _____

  _____

4. Notice who contributes to the discussion.

- Only the people included on the agenda: Yes   No
- Managers: Yes   No

  Write down their positions and names:

  _____

  _____

  _____

- Support staff: Yes   No

  Write down their positions and names:

  _____

  _____

  _____

- Consultants: Yes   No
- Others: Yes   No

5. Notice the speaking habits of group members:

  • Who speaks the most openly and inclusively? _____

    _____

  • Who speaks the most negatively? _____

  • Who uses the most jargon? _____

6. See if you can identify group roles.

  • Who is the Co-Leader? _____

  • The Skeptic? _____

  • The Mascot? _____

  • The Sycophant? _____

  • The Wallflower? _____

7. Who impressed you with his or her performance in the group? What characteristics impressed you? _____

    _____

    _____

    _____

    _____

8. Other observations: _____

    _____

    _____

    _____

    _____

Re-grouping

- A quick study of personal barometers such as body language, voice tone, and verbal context allows you to better survive in groups.

- Be ready before you enter a meeting room—make your entrance count.

- Observe the group dynamics before you plunge in. This strengthens your chances of being effective.

- Watching and listening increase your power in a group.

- Position yourself with power seating.

- The Co-Leader, The Skeptic, The Mascot, The Sycophant, and The Wallflower are all roles that emerge in groups.

three

How to Be an Active Participant

S ometimes when you're living through a long meeting, staying alert and focused can be a challenge. You'd like to be napping, reading, working—anything but trapped in this group. But you can recoup your wits and reenergize yourself by actively participating. Read on to find out how to hone your participation skills.

Your Agenda

Unless you're wearing a red-sequined jacket or a bright orange tie, getting noticed doesn't happen automatically. Having a personal agenda for every group situation helps you focus on the people who are most important to you. Your agenda also helps you pay attention and inspires you to make the most out of the time you spend in groups.

When you're part of a group, you obviously want others to notice you and appreciate your presence and contributions, but you may also have a more specific agenda. What do you want to get out of this gathering? Think of the benefits you can get from each group you're in. Think of the people you can help or who can help you:

- Do you want the vice president to notice you?
- Do you want to talk to the head of purchasing?
- Do you want to make one contribution to the meeting?
- Do you want to help the meeting end on time?

However simple or complex your agenda, jot down your goals and carry them to the meeting.

Overcoming Obstacles and Fears

Melanie is a top salesperson who makes most of her contacts and sales over the telephone. "When I get face to face with people, though, I freeze," she laments. In fact, at sales meetings her co-workers wonder what she has on the phone that's missing in the meeting room. In a gathering of professionals, Melanie acts like a lump of gum stuck on the underside of the group.

If you're like Melanie and tend to be a clam rather than a grouper, prepare for the gathering in advance. Anticipate topics of conversation and potential questions. Make notes for yourself, with quotes or comments that could be appropriate. If you still find yourself freezing up, though, or backing away from interactions, there are a couple of strategies that can help get you moving:

1. **Uphill with SLED.** Ask a friend or co-worker for support here, sharing with him or her one of your goals, such as "I want to make at least one pertinent comment during this meeting." Ask your friend to pull you along on the following SLED ride:

   - **S**it nearby. Have your friend sit next to you or across from you.

   - **L**isten actively. Ask him or her to show noticeable, active listening signs when you speak—that is to smile at you, to lean forward, to offer encouraging comments or questions.

   - **Make E**ye contact. So often you'll find that eye contact really makes a difference. Ask your friend to make eye contact with you when you talk. Look to this ally for affirmation while you're speaking, rather than at the guy who's doodling on his napkin.

   - **D**raw you in. Sometimes you have an idea but hesitate to flash it. With an aggressive group of communicators, it's often hard for the tentative to be heard. Ask your friend to draw you into the conversation so you have a chance to shine. You may want to give a signal for an area where you're prepared.

2. **CURB service.** Once you've mastered SLEDding, you're ready to add more to the group. Give your meeting CURB service with the following creative stretches:

- **Combine ideas.** To facilitate the flow and validate various contributions, look for opportunities to link similar or companionable ideas: "Joe, I hear what you said. It seems like we could combine that with Meg's suggestions and have a powerful approach to solving this issue."

- **Unlock creativity.** Use "what if" questions to enlarge and enhance the group's thinking: "What if we all took Fridays off? How would that affect the payroll costs?" Or "It sounds as though our environmental image is in jeopardy. What if we gave our star employees bus passes instead of parking places?"

  Posing "what if" questions helps your group move to a wider arena and shed conservative thinking patterns.

- **Refer to previous contributions.** Referring back to comments others have made builds synergy and goodwill. This conversation synthesizing helps people think more collectively rather than just individually.

- **Present Broad solutions.** Whenever possible, offer broad solutions that take into account as many agendas and ideas as you can. This underscores the value of participation and at the same time makes the most of the talent around the table.

Besides these specific strategies, you can power up your participation skills with these very commonsense steps:

1. **Take notes (but not too many).** Find a comfortable combination of writing and listening. Taking notes makes you look serious and helps you pay attention. However, if you're breathlessly writing every moment, you may appear overzealous and harried.

2. **Make summary comments.** When you don't have anything new to add, summarize what has been said. This flatters the speaker and helps you remember the important parts of the meeting.

3. **Ask questions that amplify or clarify.** If you don't understand a point, request an example. If you want to support a speaker, give him or her a chance to clarify or add anecdotes to the presentation. Be sensitive about time limits and the group's attention span.

4. **Keep your remarks focused and concise.** Guard the group's dynamics by modeling considerate communication tactics. Long-winded comments can blow away good group energy.

Using the "TEAM" Approach to Make Big Differences in Small Ways

"I'd love to make some changes in this group, but with my boss involved, I'm not about to mouth off on important issues."

Aaron's domineering boss has complete control of their departmental group and runs meetings like a one-man show. When you're in a situation like Aaron's, or any other where meetings aren't quite "right," don't give up. Keep alert for small ways to contribute as well as larger areas that can benefit from your fine-tuning. As an observer, use the following TEAM components to analyze the factors that affect group functioning and find areas where you can help:

Time frame

Environment

Ambiance

Members

Time frame. Are your meetings the right length? Too long and everyone gets restless and worried about work piling up. Too short, and you feel that nothing ever quite gets resolved.

Is the time of day right for this group? What times might be better for everyone? Is there a reason to meet at this particular time? How often are meetings held? Are they too often or too infrequent? Time factors have a big impact on groups, yet often, once a group gets going, people forget to notice whether the time frames are still effective.

"Our breakfast club started six years ago, with weekly meetings," says Tom. "Six years ago, the breakfast club concept was new in this area; now morning meetings are everywhere. Many of our original members are burnt out because they have so many pre-work obligations. When we looked at why we met every week, there simply wasn't a hard-and-fast reason."

Although as a participant you technically don't have "time on your hands," you can make timely suggestions to the leader. Time is one group function where you can make a difference.

Environment. Amy was orchestrating a team-building session with a group of sales reps who seldom saw each other. She rented a large room with high ceilings and lots of open space. This uncluttered spaciousness invited open communication, and the setup also gave people a chance to spread out until they got reacquainted with each other.

Beverly was organizing a similar meeting, but the only room she could get was fairly small, with tables crammed together, low ceilings, and no windows. The cramped environment did not invite joking, moving around, or risk taking. Everyone filed in, worried there would not be enough chairs. Movement was restricted and people had to sit close together. Beverly's space actively worked against the group instead of subtly advancing group members' efforts.

Environment is often overlooked. Notice how this element can add to (or detract from) the purpose of your group. A little suggestion in this area can make a big difference. Run through this mental checklist to evaluate the space where your group gets together:

☐ Is the room size right for your group?

☐ Is the temperature right? Is it too hot or too cold?

☐ Are the chairs comfortable and easy to move? Are there tables? Do you need tables? Are there barriers to honest and easy communication?

☐ Is there enough light? Is the light evenly distributed?

☐ Is the light harsh or gentle?

☐ What is the noise level? Is it distracting?

Environmental comfort is subtle and powerful. An off-putting environment affects every participant's listening and concentration.

Ambiance. Sarah and five colleagues attend night school to earn their MBAs. Since all of them are on the same track and take the same courses, they've set up a weekly study session after work. The group is a mix of managers, secretaries, and hourly people.

Sarah dreads going to these study meetings, even though she needs the support. When she walks into the break room where the meeting is held, she suddenly feels worn out, exhausted, like all the smiles have been bleached out of her. She drags herself through the session, struggling to pay attention and benefit from the group discussions.

"One evening I arrived before anyone else," she said. "As usual, I walked into the room and immediately felt the energy drain out of me. Then I realized how drab the break room was, no windows, no sense of color or excitement. I also realized too that my energy was low because I'd been sitting all day. The chairs were uncomfortable, and I was hungry."

That night, Sarah suggested they relocate to a conference room with windows and flip charts. She also suggested they take a break halfway through the session and walk in pairs through the empty corridors, discussing the material one-on-one. After the break, they shared a snack to get a "second wind."

These changes were both small and enormous. The new environment lightened the mood of the group and heightened everyone's energy. Adding food took little time but gave the participants a needed boost and a greater sense of community.

Tweaks to the ambiance and environment of your group's gatherings offer a great way to make a difference without creating a big stir. Take a minute to ask yourself the following:

☐ What is the tone of your group?

☐ Are there refreshments?

☐ Is there a mingling period before the meeting or after?

☐ Is the mood appropriate to the purpose of the group?

Members. Look at the people in your group. What gifts do they bring to the group process? What roles are they leaving out? Does the group have a cheerleader, someone who encourages and praises? Does the group have a synthesizer, someone who summarizes? Is there someone who looks out for the comfort of everyone in the group? What about a problem solver or a devil's advocate?

Don't leave yourself out of this identification process. Discover the role(s) you play and the ways you can add to the energy level of the group.

A great tool for keeping tabs on the TEAM aspects of teamwork is the checklist presented in Exercise #4. Complete the form for one of the groups you're currently involved with, or copy it and complete it for all the groups you're a member of.

Exercise #4:
TEAMworks: Areas Where I Can Make a Difference

Examine each component of the TEAM approach, considering ways you could improve one of your groups.

Group _____ Date _____

Purpose of group _____

Leader/facilitator _____

1. Timeframe

- Meeting length _____

  Suggestions _____

  _____

  Person to contact _____

  Results _____

  _____

- Time of day _____

  Suggestions _____

  _____

  Person to contact _____

  Results _____

  _____

- Frequency of meetings_____

  Suggestions _____

  _____

  Person to contact _____

  Results _____

  _____

2. Environment

- Room size _____

  Suggestions _____

  _____

  Person to contact _____

  Results _____

  _____

- Temperature _____

  Suggestions _____

  _____

  Person to contact _____

  Results _____

  _____

- Furniture (comfort and configuration) _____

  Suggestions _____

  _____

  Person to contact _____

  Results _____

  _____

- Lighting _____

  Suggestions _____

  _____

  Person to contact _____

  Results _____

  _____

3. Ambiance

- Networking or talking period (before and/or after) _____

  _____

  Suggestions _____

  _____

  Person to contact _____

  Results _____

  _____

- Refreshments _____

  Suggestions _____

  _____

  Person to contact _____

  Results _____

  _____

4. Members

- Membership mix (consider diversity of all kinds, from departmental to gender, age, and ethnicity)_____

  _____

  Suggestions _____

  _____

  Person to contact _____

  Results _____

  _____

- Personality mix _____

  Suggestions _____

  _____

  Person to contact _____

  Results _____

  _____

Taking the Plunge

You know the feeling: trapped in a group that doesn't have a competent leader who can keep the discussion moving. Someone seizes the floor, the table, indeed the very air, and begins talking for what seems like hours. The facilitator is drawing a picture of his dream house. Several other people appear to be sleeping. You have some issues to discuss and want to get into them before everyone has grown too grouchy and irritable to entertain new ideas.

What can you do?

Picture the swimming pool of your youth and remember how cold the water was in the early morning. The only way to get wet was to jump on in, right? Well, there's no way to deal with an interminable monologue in stages either—just jump in and save your fellow "droning victims" with something like this: "That's fascinating information and I'd like to hear more. I see we're running low on time and want to make sure we talk about the Adopt-a-Pet program."

If you hesitate, if you shiver and put in just a toe, if you're not confident and assertive, the talker will splash all over you!

As a participant, you have a great opportunity to learn from effective group leaders and facilitators. What works and what doesn't about how they run their groups? Study the different styles of leadership you see in your meetings and think about which combinations might work for you. Then complete Exercise #5 to organize your thoughts. Feel free to copy it for each of the meetings you attend.

Exercise #5:
Observing Your Way to the Top

As a participant, you have the unique opportunity to assess the styles of your group leaders. Learn from them what works and what doesn't when it comes to running an effective meeting.

Group _____ Date _____

Purpose of group _____

Leader/facilitator _____

1. How would you characterize the leader/facilitator's style? *(try words like gentle, inclusive, commanding, impatient, laid back, etc.)* _____

_____

_____

_____

_____

_____

2. What do you like about this style? _____

_____

_____

_____

_____

_____

3. What would make it stronger? _____

_____

_____

_____

_____

4. How does it differ from *your* natural style of leadership?

_____

_____

_____

_____

5. What would you do differently if you were in charge?

_____

_____

_____

_____

6. What can you do right now to seem more of a leader, even though you're not in charge?

_____

_____

_____

_____

Re-grouping

- Although you're not the group leader, create an agenda anyway—that is, know what you want to get personally from each meeting—so you stay purposeful and focused.

- Ask a friend in the group for support and encouragement. Ask someone you trust to listen, make eye contact, and draw you into the conversation.

- Look for areas where you can impact the group as a participant. Consider the time frame for the meeting, the environment, the ambiance, and the members' characteristics.

- Get smart and look smart during meetings. Take notes, summarize information, stay focused and concise.

- Jump in if you're in a rudderless group and try to keep the group on track.

four

Assuming Leadership in a Group

"I'm nervous about facilitating this session," Cheryl says. "I'm glad it's people I know."

"I'd rather work with strangers any day," Craig says. "They don't bring a lot of personal agendas with them."

Whether you're working with new people or a team of familiars, leading a group has its pluses and challenges. Consider how you can use the strengths of each situation and overcome the disadvantages.

In the Beginning . . .

Consider the difference between these two memos:

Memo #1:

Planning group. Tuesday 1:00 sharp. Conference room. Attendance required.

Memo #2:

Dear Program Committee Members:

It's time to create those great programs that worked so well last year. Show up at 11:30 next Wednesday for networking. Lunch starts at noon, and we'll begin our planning session at 12:30. You'll be back at your desk by 1:45. I look forward to working with you again.

The group dynamic begins at the moment you send out the memo to announce the meeting. You can enhance pre-meeting communication and attitude by tailoring your announcement to the tone and purpose of the gathering. If you're leading a brainstorming session, you don't want a didactic instructional announcement; if you're facilitating a meeting on cutbacks, you don't want something cheerful and flowery.

Before the meeting, think about the characteristics of the group. Knowing your audience helps you prepare the meeting effectively. Each meeting is like a mini-marketing campaign. You have a new product, the agenda, that you're selling to people. Before you sell this product, you need to know your audience. (Don't you love those people who call during the supper hour, wanting to sell you carpet cleaning when your entire house is hardwood floors?)

Before you bring each new group together, fill out the "Ladies and Gentlemen!" survey on the next page to find out how best to get the attention of participants and set the tone *before* the meeting.

Ladies and Gentlemen!

1. What is your relationship with the group? (Are you a boss, a co-worker, a subject matter expert, a consultant?)

   _____

2. How well do the members know each other? _____

   _____

3. Do you know every group member? _____

4. Do the members want to come to the meetings? _____

5. What do the members have in common? (Do they work in the same department, are they all artists, etc.?) _____

   _____

   • How does this help the group dynamic?_____

   _____

   • How does this hinder? _____

   _____

6. Is there a sense of team, of cooperation, here? _____

7. Is the group able to process conflict?_____

8. What is the level of commitment and participation in these meetings? _____

   _____

   What would you like it to be? _____

   _____

9. How can these meetings benefit the members? _____

_____

_____

_____

10. What do the members fear about the group process? _____

_____

_____

_____

11. Create a composite description of the group members. Be as specific as possible.

    Example:

    Sandra is a thirty-five-year-old college graduate who has worked for the company for fifteen years. She's overworked and overstressed. She does not feel empowered. She feels discriminated against because she's a woman. She comes to the meetings with the attitude, "Nobody will listen when I speak."

_____

_____

_____

_____

_____

_____

Get Ready, Get Set, Go!

"All the cattle are standing like statues," goes the song from Oklahoma! On the prairie, at the start of a beautiful morning, this is a picturesque scene. But in your meeting, if everyone stands around waiting for direction, you'll feel like you're trapped in a feedlot.

Even if you're not an experienced leader or facilitator, you can get the meeting off to a comfortable and competent start by using the "Get Ready, Get Set, Go!" method of meeting management:

> **Get Ready.** "Uh, well, we have a lot to do today and I know you're all busy. So let's get started, shall we?"

Some meetings start with all the pizzazz of a lead weight in water. Open the meeting like it matters—like your audience is a group of VIPs. Start out by grabbing their attention. Tell a story that illustrates a point. Use music to pump up the energy. Ask provocative questions. A high-energy opening shows the meeting is important to you and gets people interested in the content.

Prepare your comments like you're preparing for a speech. Have a beginning, middle, and end. Emphasize and illustrate a few important points. Make sure the ending wraps up and reiterates these points.

Get set. If group members don't know each other, think of a quick way to get everyone introduced. Creative name tags, for example, work wonders in acquainting people even before the meeting begins. Choose a topic that mirrors the gathering, provide instructions, and have participants write responses on their name tags. For instance, if you're facilitating a brainstorming session, the name tag instructions may be something like this: "List three wild ideas you'd like someone to implement."

Even if participants know each other, name tag topics can help expand their relationships. If you're leading a group session on strategic planning, the name tag suggestion might read, "What are two good business books you've recently read?"

If time permits and group interaction is important, have participants quickly introduce themselves after you've opened the meeting. You might suggest a quick topic such as this: "Say your name and tell us one part of your job you really like." Again, tailor the subject to the tone and purpose of the group.

Also at the outset, clearly express any limits and expectations:

- "We don't have a lot of time, so I need to limit discussion. I'll be available afterward to answer any questions that get left out."

- "This is a brainstorming session, so I'll expect everyone to participate. Remember, brainstorming means every idea is valid. Feel free to be wild."

This takes the guesswork out of the meeting and lets participants know what to expect.

Go! The more visual and easy to follow you make your presentation, the more people will remember. Use concrete examples that cover a variety of viewpoints, but don't imitate the following example:

"And then I single-handedly implemented the new computerization project that transformed ABC into a multinational corporation," Steve says. "After that, I moved as a consultant to help Data Dogs gain control of the canine marketplace. I engineered a program that soon will revolutionize the way business comes to our country."

Steve is a newly acquired top management specialist who is proud of his track record. He's also fascinated by his accomplishments, far more than the seventeen people desperately looking at their watches as Steve glorifies himself.

Don't use yourself in too many examples. Use the term "we" when talking about past successes. Don't tout or put down previous companies. Use pertinent examples that clarify your topic.

Are We There Yet?

Leading a meeting is like being the navigator on a trip: Sure, the map may say superhighway all the way, but when you see the sign "Road construction next forty miles," you may want to change the route. When the tank is almost empty, even if you're so close you really want to keep going, it's prudent to stop for gas.

As the leader of a group, the same conventional wisdom applies. Keep in tune with your participants so you know when they're fading away, when they're bored, or when they're traveling on their own private journey. Be prepared to speed up, change the route, or stop and let them stretch.

Give your group a structure. Let them know you're going forward, not just circling the town square.

"For a long time, I just breezed into meetings and went with the flow," says Audrey, CEO of her company and frequent leader of company meetings. "Sometimes the group was great; other times, nothing much happened. Then I began really focusing on the group and why we were gathered together. Just writing down a purpose helped me guide things along."

As the leader, you best know the direction and results you want from the group. Know where you're going and figure out how to take participants there. Before each meeting, answer the following questions:

- What is the purpose of the meeting?
- What is your agenda for the meeting?
- What tone best suits the purpose?
- How do you want participants to feel when the session is over?
- What information do you want them to walk away with?

Sharon's first act in her new position was to inform the research group that they would be taking on additional duties. "But they're already so overworked," she worried.

Because she couldn't change the purpose of the meeting or the information the group would walk away with, Sharon focused on how she wanted participants to feel when the meeting was over. She realized they wouldn't be delighted, yet she wanted them to feel hopeful and supported.

Sharon added music to the meeting and served food. She asked a member of the marketing group to come speak, as his group had already gone through the extra work syndrome and had actually flourished. She acknowledged the difficulty of what she was asking and encouraged people to talk about it in small groups, then as a whole, during the meeting. Before they left, Sharon helped the group members set up teams to deal with the additional duties they would be tackling. People left the meeting feeling hopeful and supported.

The preceding story offers a good example of focusing on what you have control over. Look at your resources. Who can help and support you? Who can add inspiration and excitement to the group? Try graphics, music, food—anything to change the tone and let people know this is not the gray-walled, humdrum meeting.

Recognizing the Cast of Characters

You met these people earlier as an observer; now you're leading them. The transformation from innocuous colleague or compliant employee to role-player is sometimes startling. Here's a review of group players with tips on how to manage them.

Yes and again yes! The Co-Leader. This informal leader supports the facilitator. He or she often answers questions readily and articulately, emphasizing points you are trying to make. The Co-Leader gives the group parameters and acknowledges contributions. Make sure this person is heard. This is someone you can consult, someone who can help you critique your meetings.

Prove it! The Skeptic. The skeptic can give you nightmares or serve as an asset—it's up to you. Try to use his or her questioning to strengthen the group and uncover points you may have forgotten. Get participants involved by having them brainstorm and wrestle with The Skeptic's objections. Don't look at this player as someone who has it in for you—rather, consider him or her as someone who's thoughtfully perusing another side of the issue.

Look at ME! The Mascot. Okay, so this person never got called on in first grade and his big sister got all the toys. Because The Mascot needs attention, figure out ways to provide some so he or she doesn't disrupt your meeting. This could take the form of a responsibility during the meeting, something that provides recognition without taking away group time.

Wonderful! The Sycophant. Everything you do is great in this player's script. Your jokes, your agenda, your every gesture make this person glow. Beware—The Sycophant may be manipulating you. Answer the praises with a genuine "thank you" and move quickly back onto the topic. Let The Sycophant know you get the message and aren't swayed by flattery.

Unplucked and Unplucky: The Wallflower. Gently ease The Wallflower out of the woodwork by talking to him or her outside your meetings. Ask: "How do you think the meeting went? I got stuck on that point about . . . How could I have handled it better?" Quietly let this player know he or she is valuable, and watch for nonthreatening ways to bring him or her out during meetings.

Leadership Ladders

How do you improve your leadership abilities? Note what went right and what felt uncomfortable at each meeting. Be candid with the group when the process falls flat. Acknowledge that you've experienced a temporary setback and share with the group how that feels. Be succinct and, unless appropriate, not too emotional. This is your chance to let people know you're flexible and imperfect, willing to learn from mistakes. It's a harmless way to model group improvement skills and gain the respect of other group members.

Recognize your problem people and track how you're dealing with them. Analyze external influences too, such as the TEAM effect (see Chapter 3). Ask a friend to critique the meetings you facilitate. Ask your group members for feedback. What would they like more of? less of?

Use your intuition to get a sense of how the group feels. Do members seem at ease? Do they seem laconic and tense? Are they interested and vivacious or watching the clock?

Sort through these impressions and use them to strengthen your style as a facilitator. In addition, seek out mentors who are wonderful with groups. Ask for their support in your quest to become at ease and elegant in your group dynamics.

Re-grouping

- Prepare for your opening remarks like you're giving a keynote speech.

- Analyze your audience and know what they need.

- Practice "Get Ready, Get Set, Go!" to get the meeting off to an effective start.

- Know the roles people tend to play in groups and use this information to strengthen your meetings.

- Leverage your leadership skills even higher with feedback from friends and with self-critique.

Weathering the Ups and Downs of Groups

The coffee is cold. The room is too small. The leader of the group arrives thirty minutes late. People are wandering in and out of the meeting, talking among themselves. Whenever and wherever groups gather, at least a million things can go wrong. Some you learn to preempt through better planning and some you learn to just ride out.

For example, you'll say things you wish you hadn't, and so will others in the group. It's all part of being a dynamic, creative team. If you realize that you "misspoke," correct your error right away: "I'm afraid I spoke too quickly and I want to clarify that last point."

On the other hand, you may have spoken quite well, but when you ask for questions you hear pens scratching, watches ticking, coffee slurping—everything but voices answering. What do you do?

Let silence work for you. Ask for questions and sit tight. Don't fidget. Don't cajole. Don't take it personally, and don't worry. You're not a hero if you break the silence too soon. If the stillness persists, smile and thank everyone for their attention.

When Thunder Rumbles and Lightning Strikes

The most difficult moments for most groups come when conflicts brew and erupt.

> *"I can't believe you called my department irresponsible!"*

> *"I said your department was behind on its monthly figures."*

> *"My department is struggling because we don't receive any support from the rest of you!"*

Sure, it would be great if everyone discussed problems in a calm and rational way, if group members would remain objective and nonjudgmental, if there was a constant feeling of camaraderie and unity. But this would also be abnormal.

Conflicts will arise. Emotions will flare. Be alert to signs of lightning on the horizon!

When you're in a group that feels like a sinking ship full of nonswimmers, simply reach out and acknowledge the discomfort: "Both of you seem to have really strong opinions and I respect both sides of the issue. Would each of you please write up the strengths of your positions for our next meeting?"

When you are the target, a similar approach works: "John, I appreciate your opinion. Would you be willing to get together and brainstorm ideas with me?" In any case, keep your emotions in check. If you need to express disappointment or other negative feelings, take a breath first and think about the best way to communicate. If you're too impassioned, people might misunderstand or not hear you clearly. Or the original point may get lost as old frustrations are revisited:

> *"I'm handling so many extra duties I can't see straight," you say. "I'd like some help around here."*

> *"Every time I ask what I can do, you say it's under control," Carla shoots back. "I joined this committee because I wanted to contribute, but I don't think you're giving me a chance."*

> *"I asked you to help make phone calls last Tuesday and you said no," you bristle.*

> *"I had a previous commitment," she says heatedly. "I asked to do it another night and you said, 'Never mind, I'll do it myself.' I think your ego is too involved in this project!"*

> *"At least I'm accomplishing things," you retort indignantly. "Last year I handled the whole fund-raising project myself and what thanks did I get for it?"*

If this sort of exchange goes on unchecked by the participants and unmediated by the leader, group energy stalls and serious damage to morale can set in. When you have a conflict with another group member, try to work it out in private rather than bringing it up with the entire group. Ask the group facilitator for help if need be.

Within the group, use "I" statements, stating the facts as you see them and your feelings. Don't blame or accuse. Don't use provocative words such as "always" and "never." Keep your remarks concise. And don't wander or change the subject. Don't add a lot of personal experiences that cloud your point.

The following "Storm Shelter" shows you how you can increase your chances of surviving stormy group situations:

State the facts. Report as exactly as possible what the person said.

"I heard you say that my department never turns in a project on time."

Test to make sure the other party agrees on the facts.

"Did I hear you correctly?"

Open up—state exactly how the other person's comments made you feel.

"When you said my department never turns in a project on time, I felt angry and upset."

Respond further by asking for resolution: say what you want to happen next.

"I'd like to schedule a meeting with a third person so we can discuss your perceptions and figure out how we can be comfortable working together."

Make sure you are heard. Ask the other party to repeat what you said. Correct any misperceptions.

Weathering Group Interactions

Any group has the possibility of sailing calm seas or becoming tempest tossed, and you don't have to be a meteorologist to predict the "weather patterns." Among members who meet regularly, you know who's typically windy and who's a relentless stream of sunshine. You know who's a storm system brewing and who embodies a polar chill.

The group's developmental stage has a lot to do with its dynamic. In any growing entity, a sense of chaos and discomfort is normal as the members of the group learn to honestly communicate and work through problems. And *communication* is definitely the key.

"The meeting went well" might mean everyone sat up straight and listened quietly. Or it may mean that Fred flew off the handle and confronted Marge, but that they worked through their issues and everyone left the group feeling bonded. When you really communicate in a group, issues are bound to arise. Learn how to recognize and defuse emotional triggers. In fact, use emotional situations to bring the group closer.

Groups go through stages. At first, participants will share polite interactions and engage in surface-level chitchat. As the group gets more deeply into the agenda, members may experience a frustration based on uncertainty about their status. Feelings of conflict may arise. A desire to avoid conflict while meeting individual and group needs then comes into play. Finally, through chaos and silence, a sense of communication and community forms.

While conflict can make you feel uncomfortable, not expressing yourself is worse. As a participant as well as a leader, you can encourage honest and open communication by simply stating the facts. Acknowledge when things get touchy by saying: "Things feel tense. I'm wondering how we can come to a resolution that meets each person's needs."

Re-grouping

- Conflict is a normal part of group interaction.
- When emotions rise, keep cool by recognizing your feelings and not accusing anyone.
- Accept your mistakes and own them.
- Learn to let silence work for you.

six

Growing Into Group Greatness

"Let's have lunch sometime."

"Lunch with Dee, Tuesday, 11:45, The Classic Cup."

"I really want to take a course in communication."

"Wednesday morning, call the university and order a course catalog."

"That sounds like a great idea. We'll have to get together and work on it."

"Saturday, 3:00 p.m. at Denny's. Brainstorming session with Cindy, Anne, and Judith."

The more concrete and scheduled your goals, the better chance you have to make them into realities. However, most of us pay more attention to our calendars than to our goals. Now is the time to combine the two and forge concrete steps for your foray into group greatness.

Review your self-portrait from Chapter 1. Have you added groups? Have you thought of other groups you go to? Have you eliminated groups?

Review your goals for the three stress-free groups you identified. Have you achieved these goals? Have you achieved others? Were you too shy to try or too busy to care?

Analyze your groups and see where you can really make a difference, to yourself, to your career, and to the group. First, rate your groups to see which will give you the most bang for your efforts. Then, complete the "Getting Greater" form in Exercise #6 for at least three to five groups that are important to you. This format will help you objectify and clarify your opportunities for change with each group.

Exercise #6:
Getting Greater

To understand how to best use your time and energy, analyze your opportunities with each of your most important groups. Fill in this sheet for at least three to five important groups.

Name of group _____

   A. Circle the most appropriate answer:

      1. Meeting times:

         Weekly   Bi-weekly   Monthly

         Quarterly   As Needed   Other

      2. Size:

         Less than 5   5 to 10

         11 to 20   More than 20

      3. Your role in this group:

         Leader   Active participant   Passive participant

      4. This group affects your (choose as many as are applicable):

         Job   Career   Client base

         Potential for promotion

         Information base

         Relationships with clients

         Relationship with co-workers

         Other

5. In this group you have opportunities to participate:

   Very   Frequently   Seldom   Hah!

6. You have allies and supporters in this group:

   Yes   I don't know   No

B. After completing these pictures of several groups, look at your responses and choose three groups to focus on. Complete the following questions for each:

   1. List the greatest things that could happen to you in this group.

      Examples:

      - "I became the leader of the group and they asked me to represent them at the national conference in San Francisco."

      - "I figured out how to get everyone comfortable with each other."

      _____

      _____

      _____

      Let go of rational thinking and really dream. Make a list on a separate piece of paper. Look at the great things and combine and refine until you come up with a goal statement for the group.

   2. Your goal: "Wouldn't it be great if..."

      _____

      _____

3. List your allies and the ways they might help:

   Ally   Assistance

   1. _____   _____

   2. _____   _____

4. Take your big goal and break it up into small steps.

   Example:

   Goal: Get everyone in the group interacting and getting along

   First steps: Talk to Rita from purchasing

   _____

   _____

   _____

5. Feedback:

   What happened? _____

   What went right? _____

   What could be better? _____

   What would I do differently next time? _____

After each group gathering, have a mini-celebration for yourself when things go well. You are changing patterns, creating a new social self. You are taking charge in a new and powerful way. This is big stuff!

After a month, reevaluate your goals and see how you're doing. Celebrate the small victorious steps, and realign and redesign the larger goal if you need to.

Bibliography and Suggested Reading

Alessandra, Tony, and Phil Hunsaker. *Communicating at Work*. New York: Simon & Schuster, 1993.

Caroselli, Marlene. *Meetings That Work*. Mission, KS: SkillPath Publications, 1994.

Glass, Lillian. *Say It Right*. New York: Perigree, 1991.

Haynes, Marian. *Effective Meeeting Skills*. Menlo Park, CA: Crisp, 1988.

Shouse, Deborah. *NameTags Plus*. Mission, KS: SkillPath Publications, 1995.

Available From
SkillPath Publications

Self-Study Sourcebooks

Climbing the Corporate Ladder: What You Need to Know and Do to Be a Promotable Person *by Barbara Pachter and Marjorie Brody*

Coping With Supervisory Nightmares: 12 Common Nightmares of Leadership and What You Can Do About Them *by Michael and Deborah Singer Dobson*

Defeating Procrastination: 52 Fail-Safe Tips for Keeping Time on Your Side *by Marlene Caroselli, Ed.D.*

Discovering Your Purpose *by Ivy Haley*

Going for the Gold: Winning the Gold Medal for Financial Independence *by Lesley D. Bissett, CFP*

Having Something to Say When You Have to Say Something: The Art of Organizing Your Presentation *by Randy Horn*

Info-Flood: How to Swim in a Sea of Information Without Going Under *by Marlene Caroselli, Ed.D.*

The Innovative Secretary *by Marlene Caroselli, Ed.D.*

Mastering the Art of Communication: Your Keys to Developing a More Effective Personal Style *by Michelle Fairfield Poley*

Obstacle Illusions: Coverting Crisis to Opportunity *by Marlene Caroselli, Ed.D.*

Organized for Success! 95 Tips for Taking Control of Your Time, Your Space, and Your Life *by Nanci McGraw*

A Passion to Lead! How to Develop Your Natural Leadership Ability *by Michael Plumstead*

P.E.R.S.U.A.D.E.: Communication Strategies That Move People to Action *by Marlene Caroselli, Ed.D.*

Productivity Power: 250 Great Ideas for Being More Productive *by Jim Temme*

Promoting Yourself: 50 Ways to Increase Your Prestige, Power, and Paycheck *by Marlene Caroselli, Ed.D.*

Proof Positive: How to Find Errors Before They Embarrass You *by Karen L. Anderson*

Risk-Taking: 50 Ways to Turn Risks Into Rewards *by Marlene Caroselli, Ed.D. and David Harris*

Stress Control: How You Can Find Relief From Life's Daily Stress *by Steve Bell*

The Technical Writer's Guide *by Robert McGraw*

Total Quality Customer Service: How to Make It Your Way of Life *by Jim Temme*

Write It Right! A Guide for Clear and Correct Writing *by Richard Andersen and Helene Hinis*

Your Total Communication Image *by Janet Signe Olson, Ph.D.*

Handbooks

The ABC's of Empowered Teams: Building Blocks for Success *by Mark Towers*

Assert Yourself! Developing Power-Packed Communication Skills to Make Your Points Clearly, Confidently, and Persuasively *by Lisa Contini*

Breaking the Ice: How to Improve Your On-the-Spot Communication Skills
by Deborah Shouse

The Care and Keeping of Customers: A Treasury of Facts, Tips, and Proven Techniques for Keeping Your Customers Coming BACK! *by Roy Lantz*

Challenging Change: Five Steps for Dealing With Change *by Holly DeForest and Mary Steinberg*

Dynamic Delegation: A Manager's Guide for Active Empowerment *by Mark Towers*

Every Woman's Guide to Career Success *by Denise M. Dudley*

Grammar? No Problem! *by Dave Davies*

Great Openings and Closings: 28 Ways to Launch and Land Your Presentations With Punch, Power, and Pizazz *by Mari Pat Varga*

Hiring and Firing: What Every Manager Needs to Know *by Marlene Caroselli, Ed.D. with Laura Wyeth, Ms.Ed.*

How to Be a More Effective Group Communicator: Finding Your Role and Boosting Your Confidence in Group Situations *by Deborah Shouse*

How to Deal With Difficult People *by Paul Friedman*

Learning to Laugh at Work: The Power of Humor in the Workplace *by Robert McGraw*

Making Your Mark: How to Develop a Personal Marketing Plan for Becoming More Visible and More Appreciated at Work *by Deborah Shouse*

Meetings That Work *by Marlene Caroselli, Ed.D.*

The Mentoring Advantage: How to Help Your Career Soar to New Heights
by Pam Grout

Minding Your Business Manners: Etiquette Tips for Presenting Yourself Professionally in Every Business Situation *by Marjorie Brody and Barbara Pachter*

Misspeller's Guide *by Joel and Ruth Schroeder*

Motivation in the Workplace: How to Motivate Workers to Peak Performance and Productivity *by Barbara Fielder*

NameTags Plus: Games You Can Play When People Don't Know What to Say
by Deborah Shouse

Networking: How to Creatively Tap Your People Resources *by Colleen Clarke*

New & Improved! 25 Ways to Be More Creative and More Effective *by Pam Grout*

Power Write! A Practical Guide to Words That Work *by Helene Hinis*

The Power of Positivity: Eighty ways to energize your life
by Joel and Ruth Schroeder

Putting Anger to Work For You *by Ruth and Joel Schroeder*

Reinventing Your Self: 28 Strategies for Coping With Change *by Mark Towers*

Saying "No" to Negativity: How to Manage Negativity in Yourself, Your Boss, and Your Co-Workers *by Zoie Kaye*

The Supervisor's Guide: The Everyday Guide to Coordinating People and Tasks
by Jerry Brown and Denise Dudley, Ph.D.

Taking Charge: A Personal Guide to Managing Projects and Priorities
by Michal E. Feder

Treasure Hunt: 10 Stepping Stones to a New and More Confident You! *by Pam Grout*

A Winning Attitude: How to Develop Your Most Important Asset!
by Michelle Fairfield Poley

For more information, call 1-800-873-7545.

Notes

Notes

Notes

Notes

Notes

Notes

Notes

Notes

Notes

Notes

Notes

Notes

Notes

Notes